IN 30 DAYS

Elizabeth Levang
and Curtis Levang, Ph.D

CompCare® Publishers
2415 Annapolis Lane
Minneapolis, MN 55441

ISBN: 0-89638-296-6

Cover Design by Barry Littmann

Inquiries, orders and catalog requests should be sent to
CompCare Publishers
2415 Annapolis Lane
Minneapolis, Minnesota 55441
Call toll free 800/328-3330
or 612/559-4800

BECOME A BETTER LOVER IN 30 DAYS

Ingredients for Loving

Paul and Karen sat across from each other at the breakfast table, eating in sleepy silence. Paul gazed tiredly at the financial section of the newspaper, and Karen studied the corn flakes box. Suddenly Karen's face brightened.

"New and improved," she murmured, smiling.

"Huh?"

"Our relationship," Karen explained. "I think it could stand some improvement too."

Most relationships, like Paul and Karen's, don't explode in an anger-filled holocaust. Instead they grow stale and soggy—like corn flakes in milk. Just as corn flakes lose their appeal after soaking forever in the same old colorless milk, a relationship can lose its passion after months or years of sameness.

When that happens it's not time to throw out the package and start over. You can become a better lover, not by wholesale change, but by varying some of the ingredients. Here are the ingredients we believe can make your love relationship new and improved.

1. Decide to be a lover once again.
Resolve to make a change. If you want to be a better lover, make a commitment to that goal.

2. Start thinking like a lover.
Early in your relationship, acting like a lover probably took little effort. It's time to renew that habit of making love. Make it your first priority.

3. Act like a lover.
When was the last time you spent an evening alone, shared a quiet dinner, or gave each other a back rub? Now's the time to give your love life a jump start.

4. Live like a lover.
With regular attention and a touch of imagination you can revive romance, passion, and desire. You can live the lifestyle of a lover.

TODAY

Put your imagination to work. Take a hot bath today or find a quiet place to be alone with your thoughts. As you're relaxing, think about things you can do to start being an ideal lover.

Fresh Starts

If someone asked you to describe exactly what you saw on your drive to work today, do you think you could recall even 20 percent of what you saw? After a while of traveling over the same familiar roads, our mind seems to just tune out what's around us.

Our relationships are no different. Most of us don't even wait for our partners to finish speaking before we jump in and finish their sentences for them. Likewise, we don't remember what they wore this morning or whether they were on foot or horseback. We've stopped listening and paying attention because we're so accustomed to their routines and habits.

To be a better lover, start fresh and begin observing things as if they were new. This means discarding old prejudices and acting as if your partner is a Nobel Prize winner, a glamour model, or some famous dignitary rather than the person who cleans our toilet or belches at the dinner table. The point is to take a new look that is free of past assumptions.

For the moment, act as if what your partner says and does is the most interesting and fascinating thing you have heard. Being curious allows us to learn something new because, after all, our partner has probably changed some since we last checked.

Another helpful piece is to stop asking yes-or-no questions and try the fill-in-the-blank type. Getting beyond one-word answers may be like sticking your hand into a grab bag: you don't know what you'll pull out, but it's sure to be a surprise.

TODAY

Sit face to face with your partner, with your eyes closed. Imagine you are on an expedition, looking for hidden treasure. Massage your partner's face, arm, neck, and hands. What treasures do you uncover?

DAY 3

Let Go of Old Hurts

It seems that the more we love and care about someone, the greater our chance of feeling hurt by something that person says or does. In fact, if we didn't care, we probably wouldn't get disappointed. To stop caring is not the answer. Instead, we must strive to not allow small disappointments to divide us and spoil our relationship.

We need to regularly give vent to life's little frustrations. This works best when we keep a sense of humor and play fair. Playing fair means not adding fuel to the fire or hitting below the belt. It means not using words like "always" or "never" to criticize your partner's actions. It means avoiding blaming and shaming to "beat" your partner into submission. After all, if you view your partner as your opponent, you will have very little chance of being winning players on the same team.

Let go of old resentments and set aside bitterness so you can both move on. Realize that although life

8

may not always give you as much as you feel you deserve, you can be just as happy with other, unexpected gifts whose real value may not be obvious at the time. Let go of the idea that life must always turn out exactly as you had planned it, and open yourself to the possibility that you and your partner can create your lives anew together each day.

TODAY

Lighten your load. Make a list of the resentments you have stored up toward your partner. Take a drive to the nearest party supply store and buy a helium-filled balloon. Tie your list of resentments to the string and let it go sailing away.

DAY 4 ────────────

Crazy in Love

Most of us have experienced the giddy feeling of falling headlong in love—the dizzying, butterflies-in-the-stomach, clammy-hands feeling of being crazy in love. We remember the rush of emotions we felt when we saw each other or talked together after a period of separation. We recall the ache we felt when we were apart and the anxiety we felt when we feared that our love would not be returned.

Falling in love again does not have to be all that difficult. It can happen by looking at things with a fresh eye and a loving, willing heart. People fall in love for all sorts of reasons. We're charmed by the mischief in someone's eyes or enchanted by someone's sense of humor. The sparks that started our engine and first attracted us to each other can be our key to falling in love with our partners again.

When we think back to our dating period, our first kiss, our special song, loving moments, and the fun things we used to do, we clear away the cobwebs and come back to those essential elements that nurtured our love. If walking in the park, riding horses, going to movies, or roasting hot dogs in the fireplace were what forged our bond, great! Start doing these things again. If we were attracted to our partners because of their fascinating conversation or their surefootedness on the dance floor, encourage these aspects. Ask them to retell a favorite story or show you how to do the foxtrot.

You don't have to start over at square one. By remembering, you can find the specialness that was yours then and still is.

TODAY

Play a game of "Remember When...." Dig out your old photo albums and pull out a few special pictures. Post them in conspicuous places—on the bathroom mirror, on a bed pillow, on the refrigerator, on the dashboard of the car, and other places. As you look at the pictures, try to remember what you felt like when they were taken. Immerse yourself in feelings from the past; let them wash over you.

Commitment

When our nephew was a youngster, he wanted a puppy more than anything. It was all Bryce could talk about. Over and over, he promised his parents how much he would love and take care of a puppy. It would be the best present he could ever have.

After Bryce had his puppy for a while, Mom and Dad were the ones cleaning up the messes and doing all the things young Bryce had promised to be responsible for.

Sometimes nurturing a relationship is like having a pet: we've pledged to stick together through thick and thin, yet after a while the newness may wear off and our enthusiasm wanes. When those inevitable messes occur, we might not be sure we can muster the energy or practice the skills we need to fix them.

Commitment is a choice that must be regularly reviewed and renewed. Commitment means holding your tongue or apologizing first, not threatening divorce after every argument. It means seeing your partner's point of view even though you want to defend your own stance. It means sticking up for your partner when your family or friends find fault.

Loving someone is definitely risky business, for there is no guarantee that our feelings will be returned. Committed love is not for the faint-hearted.

What makes it all worthwhile is that special feeling we get when we are nestled in bed like two spoons in the kitchen drawer. Or when our partner says he or she still believes in us despite our getting turned down for a job we really wanted.

We might not get everything we want in love, but by going after our heart's desire with all our might, we give ourselves a fighting chance.

TODAY

If you are married, read your wedding vows aloud, feeling the weight and importance of each word. If you are in a different type of committed relationship, repeat your commitment ritual or make up a new one together to renew your love. Seal your love with a kiss.

DAY 6
Trust

Having trust in our partner gives him or her the opportunity to respond with honesty and to be more self-disclosing. It also makes it much easier for our partner to take responsibility for his or her actions without being defensive.

One Saturday, after working around the house for several hours, Ray sat down to rest. Just at that moment Sara came by carrying an armful of dirty laundry. Assuming Ray was goofing off, Sara began complaining about all the work she was doing and how unfair Ray was being by just sitting on his duff, doing nothing. Ray tried to defend himself by listing all the things he had been doing that day.

Before things got out of hand, the couple were able to see how their distrust of each other had put the torpedoes in the launch position. Sara had not given Ray the benefit of the doubt.

More often than not, we focus on our lovers' shortcomings rather than their thoughtfulness and kindness. All too commonly couples complain about having done fifteen things right and then being blown out of the water by making one small slip. They can feel that all their good efforts are wasted.

Playing our cards differently can make an important difference. Rather than leading with an accusation, judgment, or criticism, we can open with a "trust" card. That means giving our partners the benefit of the doubt by assuming that their intentions were positive and that they were acting in good faith.

TODAY

Get two 3 x 5-inch index cards. Write "I trust you" on one card and "I want to trust you" on another. Hand them to your partner whenever you want to show that you are giving your partner the benefit of the doubt or trying your very best.

Live as Adults

Shortly after they were married, Sam and Georgia bought a piece of lakeshore property and built a small house. Sam thoroughly enjoyed living on the lake. In the summer he fished and swam, and in the winter he skied and tobogganed. Because of all his talk of such a terrific life, Sam's mother, Val, found a house four doors down and moved in to the neighborhood.

Because Georgia was out of town quite a bit, Val regularly stopped by to straighten up things around the house and leave home-cooked meals for Sam. These actions grew to be just enough to sink Sam's boat.

Sam decided to finally cut his mother loose and get on with his own life. Sam bought his mother a blank card and wrote the following note inside: "I love you, Mother, for all the wonderful things you did for me as a boy. Although I will always be your son, now I am a man and I must live as a man. Thank you for letting Georgia and me fashion our life together, however crude it may seem."

Sometimes parents have a hard time letting go of their children, and vice versa. Those with the strongest and longest apron strings often worry that they won't be able to survive. Yet sooner or later we all need to let go if our own, adult love relationships are to survive. Cutting the apron strings frees us to truly love and be loved.

TODAY

Whatever ghosts or goblins you're holding onto—your parents, your adult children, a previous relationship—finally send them packing. Take any unused cardboard box and several sheets of paper. On each sheet, write down any old pieces of emotional baggage you've been hauling around with you. Put the pages into the box, wrap the box in brown paper, and toss it into the trash can.

Lovable You

How lovable do you feel? Being in love is one thing; being lovable is another. It's the difference between how we feel about someone else and how we feel about ourselves.

Men often measure their "lovability" by how successful they are and how much money they've made or prestige they've gained. Women tend to evaluate their lovability in terms of their physical attractiveness. These yardsticks have a built-in problem, however. By comparing ourselves to others, we fail to take into account our own accomplishments and uniqueness.

If you're naturally diminutive, you'll probably never look like one of those towering beauties that grace the magazine covers or those Adonis types in muscle magazines. And why assume that's what your partner wants anyway?

Thinking of ourselves as less than lovable makes it hard, if not impossible, for our lover to get close to us. Our negative actions and attitudes toward ourselves set up all kinds of roadblocks and barriers to love.

We can begin to believe we are unlovable for many reasons: being pregnant and feeling "fat," having a "perfect" mother-in-law come to visit, losing an important account at work, or finding fifteen gray hairs. Whatever the reason, it's important to see things in their proper perspective and to be more realistic about life.

If we measure our lovability in terms of how much money we make, how new our car is, or whether we rent or own our home, we need to change the way we think. In the long run, material things don't matter. They only wear out or fall apart. What sustains us throughout life is the love we give ourselves and those close to us.

TODAY

Reflect on the inner qualities that attracted you to your partner. Appreciate yourself; see yourself the way your partner saw you when you first became lovers.

Friendship

At times in your relationship, you probably have considered your partner to be your best friend. You could talk about anything and everything and you always understood. Everything you had you shared, and being together meant the world to you.

Although time may have changed your relationship in ways that are not necessarily healthy, you can reclaim what you and your partner had in the past. What made you best friends and helped to cement your friendship still exists.

Friendships are based largely on mutual interests. At one time you probably liked the same sports, were interested in the same social causes, attended the same concerts, and had the same friends. For whatever reason, life brought you into the same room at the same time and presto—your friendship and love relationship developed.

To recapture your friendship, get to know each other again. This means spending some time alone just talking, sharing, and discovering what common ground you still have. Doing this in small doses of about fifteen minutes a day is best in the beginning. Just getting your feet wet rather than jumping in altogether eases the pressure initially and lets you rediscover those interests and ideas that once brought you together.

TODAY

Find a TV show or movie you both want to see. Watch it together. Later on, discuss things you liked and disliked about it. Or, if books are more your style, choose one you both want to read and schedule an hour before bedtime to read it to one another. Consider doing so every night.

Expectations

Wouldn't you love to go on a long, unhurried vacation to a tropical island, double your salary overnight, or be able to sleep until noon every weekend? Most of us would probably give a resounding yes to these things.

There is a vast difference between the essential things we need to survive and the things that would make our lives more comfortable and pleasurable. When we get in the business of confusing wants with needs, we usually feel we're being unfairly treated and deprived. Oftentimes we place unrealistic expectations on our partners and on ourselves.

It's important to tell ourselves that when we don't get what we want, it may be unpleasant or disappointing, but it won't devastate us.

It would be nice to make love more often, to be a size eight and fit into that sexy bikini, or to feel like the star quarterback on a winning team. But there's more to love than glitz and glamour.

Take note of what's available to you today. Though it may need some improving, you do have a relationship. Each day you can do a number of small things to become a better lover.

Taking the time to nuzzle an ear, massage tired shoulders, or give an unexpected peck on the cheek shows how interested you are in your partner. Likewise, calling from work just to say "hi" or whipping up a silly homemade card lets your partner know you are thinking of him or her even when you're away.

TODAY

Declare today Princess or Prince Day and treat your partner like royalty. Make your partner's every wish your command.

DAY 11

Celebrate Life with Your Partner

Has one of you ever accused the other of sleepwalking through your relationship? If your partner has been sleepwalking his or her way through your life together, you probably feel ignored or discounted. If you want to be a better lover, become aware of ways you can express your appreciation to your partner. Here's our list of do's and don'ts:

- Do admit when you are overloaded or preoccupied and unable to listen. Schedule time to listen to your partner.

- Don't pretend to be paying attention to your lover when your mind is really elsewhere.

- Do nice things for each other, without expecting anything in return.

- Don't expect to be rewarded for every nice thing you do for your partner; be loving simply to be loving.

- Do call just to say "I love you" or "I miss you."

- Don't underestimate the importance of little things.

- Do recognize all those important birthdays, anniversaries, and holidays—especially Valentine's Day.

- Don't forget to celebrate life's milestone events by sending cards, flowers, or a small gift; it needn't be extravagant.

- Do notice your partner's efforts and progress towards improving appearance, attitude, or disposition.

- Don't ignore opportunities to shower your partner with compliments.

TODAY

Send flowers to your partner for no reason other than to say "I love you."

DAY 12
The Gift of Sexuality

People come in all shapes and sizes, from small to large to everything in between. There are loud people, quiet people, nudists, Buddhists, and prudists.

Some like lingering sex, quickie sex, or special-occasion-only sex. Some like making love with the shades drawn; others like their lovemaking sunny side up.

There are no universals or standards when it comes to matters of sexuality. Our preferences and our tastes don't matter in the least. What matters is being comfortable with ourselves and respectful of our lovers' needs.

To get more comfortable with your sexuality, you may need to replace confusing and negative messages from the past with new, clear images of your own making. Think of yourself as gorgeous, desirable, and sexy, no matter what size, shape, or condition you are in.

Think about sexuality as a gift to be appreciated

and celebrated. It's exciting to think of ourselves as the sexual beings that we are. Take pride in the fact that you want to be a good lover. Enjoy feeling lusty and a little zany in the process.

There are countless loving ways to nurture and encourage each other's sexuality. Tell your partner how much he turns you on. Let your partner know you love the way she looks, feels, and tastes. The more you boost each other's sexual confidence, the more you both will benefit.

TODAY

The next time you make love, remind your partner how much you enjoy the way he or she looks, feels, tastes, smells. You can express your appreciation in many ways—through touch, kisses, or conversation. Ask your partner what he or she would find most pleasing; then do it!

Love's Small Pleasures

How often do you find items like these on your "To Do" list:

> Snuggle all night on the couch.
> Make out in the car.
> Play footsy under the dinner table.
> Have breakfast in bed.

Andy Rooney might say, "Did you ever wonder why people spend so much time being busy and so little time being in love?" Life is full of distractions, and those who take time to have fun and be intimate are often scorned as being lazy, selfish, or just plain nuts.

Switch from working for pay to working for love. Put your time, energy, and lips in gear. Why not make a new "To Do" list with our lover as the number-one priority. Sound silly? So what? It's time to reclaim what is important.

To make love a priority, begin anticipating your lover's needs and wants. Actively begin to be thoughtful and caring; don't worry that you may be off the mark. How about bringing home your partner's favorite candy bar and feeding it to him or her bite by bite, waking him up in the morning with a hot, steamy washcloth, or brushing and stroking her hair at the end of the day.

A lover needs to know that he or she is important to us, rating top bunk in your heart. Pay attention to small things that make your partner feel on top of the world.

TODAY

Buy yourself a new notebook. On the first page, write "Top Priority: Love" across the top. List three to five loving actions and carry out at least two of them. Add to this list throughout the week.

DAY 14

Criticism

Some things almost always prevent people from becoming good lovers. Common culprits are hurtful words, actions, attitudes, and even gestures that communicate unloving, unproductive criticism. Unkind criticism wounds the spirit and sends one's feelings of self-worth plummeting.

Cutting remarks, put-downs, and slams are all ways of criticizing someone. No man appreciates it when his partner invites his co-workers to dinner and then announces that he has performance problems at home, too, not just at the office. The savvy woman uses praise—not put-downs—in front of her partner's associates. And no woman appreciates being told that she is not as slim and sexy as she was when she was younger.

Couples sometimes forget that criticisms leveled in the morning may come back to haunt them at bedtime. What we say and how we say it are important. Criticism is like a boomerang; what we toss out is sure to come back to us.

TODAY

Do you know what criticisms your partner finds especially harsh and painful? Do you try to avoid using your partner's vulnerabilities against him or her during a disagreement? If you're not sure of the answers to these questions, you may be hurting your partner without realizing it. Ask your lover to inform you privately when you offend him or her. Be kind to your partner when it seems most difficult to do so—during your next disagreement.

Signal Your Love

Over the years Ken and Sandy developed a number of signals to telegraph their interest in making love. Sandy's favorite trick was to don a flaming red leather skirt and flirt with Ken with statements like "I'm a red-hot fire. Feel the heat of my flames!"

Ken's approach was a bit simpler, yet just as effective. He would sort through his albums and pull out a certain golden-oldie favorite. He would set it spinning on the turntable and croon along.

Ken and Sandy's signals were a subtle invitation. They knew what the signals meant and they were free to play along or not. The fact that their actions were playful led to sex that was spontaneous and exciting rather than predictable and obligatory.

Writing notes, flirting outrageously with not-so-subtle verbal signals, wearing sexy clothing, or even using a simple gesture such as massaging your partner's earlobe are all ways of letting your partner know when you're in the mood for love.

Best of all, these signals and codes are your unique and private love language. Your kids, friends, and relatives need never catch on.

Whether verbal or nonverbal, your love language fortifies the special bond between you and keeps your relationship fresh and alive.

TODAY

Think of new ways to communicate your desire for love to your partner. What would excite your lover the most? Sexy outfits or lingerie? Telling your lover over the phone how much you want to make love when you next see each other? Try to delight your partner and yourself tonight with something new and a bit wild.

Listen with Your Heart

When you were dating, you probably enjoyed spending hours on the telephone or talking until the wee hours. Now sometimes it's a challenge to find even one or two interesting things to say to each other. What happened?

When your relationship was new, you were eager to learn everything about each other. You talked as a way to get closer, and you were bent on listening. The more you talked and listened, the closer you became.

Now you may be smothering your conversations with wet blankets. You can put a damper on love with statements like "Not that dumb story again, honey," or "Let's not talk about that now!" As sure as throwing water on a fire, statements like these douse the flames of love and passion.

Here are a few ways you turn back the clock and learn to enjoy each other's company again. Start by sharpening up your listening skills. If you really want to shock your partner, try repeating or paraphrasing his or her conversation now and then. The idea is to acknowledge what you've heard and not argue or change the subject.

Your goal is to show your partner that you are truly listening and paying attention. When your partner realizes you are truly listening, he or she may open up and talk about things not discussed in a long time. Why would this be so? Because your partner feels heard, understood, and valued.

Remember the simple rules of staying in conversation with your partner:

1. No wet blankets.

2. Use your best listening skills.

3. Spend ample time talking and listening, even if it means staying up late.

TODAY

Actively listen to your partner—that is, with your heart as well as your ears. Try to put yourself in your partner's place and understand what he or she is feeling during the conversation. Repeat this exercise daily for the rest of the week.

Sexual Needs

Some of us fulfill our needs for love and intimacy strictly through sex. Others view the sexual act as only one of many ways to be intimate. Whatever the case, what's important is feeling satisfied sexually.

A guaranteed way to feel more fulfilled and satisfied sexually is to focus on quality. This does not mean becoming a contortionist so that we can make love while standing on one foot in the shower. Nor does it mean that the number of times we make love in a month has to equal the number of channels we have on our cable TV.

What it does mean is telling our partners what our sexual needs are. Communicate when you want to be cuddled, fondled, pampered, seduced, or kissed from head to toe. Let your partner know how much of this you want at a given time.

Likewise, we need to open ourselves to our lovers' needs and be willing to give as well as receive.

Buying a sexy nightgown, trying out a great new

cologne, or setting a seductive mood in the bedroom by replacing plain lightbulbs with colored ones are good mood enhancers. Even nicer is the message that goes along with these actions: your partner's sexual needs matter, and so do yours.

TODAY

Ask your partner to tell you if you have been satisfying his or her sexual needs. Are there fantasies the two of you have not shared? If you need help recognizing your own or your partner's needs, the public library is an excellent resource for literature—from textbook clinical to erotic!

DAY 18
Look Your Best

Given a choice, we would tend to choose a package
that's neatly wrapped and secured with a colorful bow
rather than one wrapped in brown paper and tied up
with string. The fact is, our appearance plays an
important part in creating sexual attraction and setting the mood for love.

If you've been neglecting your appearance lately,
set aside some time to make yourself look your very
best! If you haven't shaved for a couple of days, get
out that shaver, insert a fresh blade, and have a shaving party. Let your partner lather you up and whisk
off that stubble. Emergency rooms are not strewn with
the hacked-up faces of men whose partners have
wielded a safety razor.

By the same token, if you've let bathing slip by,
draw a hot bath, fill the water with fragrant bubble
bath, and jump in. A good soak and soap will prove
stimulating for more than one reason—especially if
your partner joins you.

When was the last time you had your hair trimmed, colored, or styled? Salons from inexpensive to ultra-chic are as plentiful these days as fast-food restaurants. Ease back into the barber chair and let your stylist use your natural assets to help you look your very best. Add a stylish shirt or outfit, a dab of makeup or cologne, and voilà!

TODAY

Treat your partner and yourself to a day at the spa. Go for the works! If the cost of a professional spa is prohibitive, create your own spa at home. Treat each other to relaxing herbal baths, body rubs with fragrant oils, manicures, pedicures, and hair styling. Then dress for a night on the town and dance the night away.

DAY 19

Treat Your Partner Like a Guest

Before company comes over, most of us spend time tidying up the house and getting ourselves ready. We pick up the newspapers littering the living room, make sure there are clean guest towels in the bathroom, and polish the flatwear till it gleams. We take time to comb our hair, put on a clean pair of pants or outfit, tuck in our shirt, and freshen our lipstick. Our guests are special, and we want to make a good impression on them.

On the other hand, when it's "just" the family, we feel there's no one to impress, so comfortable and casual is the order of the day. Who needs makeup, a clean shirt, or a close shave?

Think about how backwards all this is: we fuss more over guests—relative strangers—than over our own family members who so enrich our lives.

Turn the tables permanently and begin treating your partner like a guest. Those things you routinely do for guests, now do for your partner. Help make your partner comfortable at the end of the day, say "please" and "thank you," listen attentively, and instead of arguing when you disagree, respond respectfully.

When you see your lover as an important person and make him or her a priority, you will be surprised how much closer and more intimate you feel.

TODAY

Stage a private dinner with your partner. Splurge on the menu; serve foods both you and your partner love. Use your best dishes and flatware. Light some candles and put on some favorite romantic music.

Try New Things

Most of us would probably have trouble remembering everywhere we went and everything we did last week or even yesterday. After a while, the days tend to seem so similar it's as if they've all been stamped out by the same cookie cutter.

If complacency and routine have taken over your days, put some spontaneity back into your life. The key to spontaneity is taking advantage of any opportunities that come your way. When you take advantage of opportunities, you can go from boredom to excitement.

Start noticing those opportunities that let you do something out of the ordinary, something you would never pay to do or plan to do. If your boss or someone else you know offers you free tickets to a mud-wrestling match, a charity event, or a play, take them and run. Even if you don't particularly care for the event, you've been given a good reason to get out of your rut and do something exciting and different. And since someone else is picking up the tab, you've got nothing to lose.

Likewise, if the kids go off to the movies with friends or take an unexpected nap on Saturday afternoon, don't hustle about catching up on yard work or house work. Slip your partner a note that says, "Meet me in five." Then draw the curtains or pull down the blinds, turn on some soft, romantic music, spray a touch of perfume or cologne on the pillows, and glide under the sheets.

The truth is that it takes just as much effort to complain as it does to change. Life is boring only because we let it get boring. In the same way, life can be exciting if we put a little effort into making things different.

TODAY

Plan some time alone. Look in the newspaper for an event you wouldn't normally attend. It can be anything from a ballet to a tractor pull. Get two tickets, grab your partner, and go!

Aging

Jim no longer feels like the virile, energetic lover he once believed he was. These days he'd just as soon watch a love scene on TV as participate in one. Truthfully, Jim feels a little guilty because he doesn't want to make love as often as his wife does.

Sexual desires change from adolescence to early adulthood to late adulthood. It is not unusual for women to desire sex more frequently as they get older, particularly when they are no longer worried about becoming pregnant. Fortunately, the older we get, the less we need to prove sexually that we are a "real" man or woman. And as the kids get older and we become more secure financially, we have fewer distractions and more opportunities for lovemaking.

Physical changes are a normal part of aging, and being a good lover means adapting to those changes. Lovemaking may take a little extra time for us as our engines may need to warm up longer to get those juices running or that piston pumping. And some of the things we used to enjoy physically may not bring us as much satisfaction today.

On the other hand, our personalities may change somewhat too. Once timid or unsure in our lovemaking, we may become more like a tiger than the lamb that we used to be.

It's best to accept our bodies as they are and adjust our expectations according to the natural and normal changes that come with age. Like a good bottle of wine, things often improve with age.

TODAY

Make a list of things that get better as they get older. No idea is too far out. A couple of ideas to start your list are wine and memories.

DAY 22

Be Sensitive

Most of us notice the subtle changes that indicate when something's gone wrong with our car. There's that funny knocking and pinging sound, that difficulty we have accelerating, or that loose door handle. These are signals that the engine needs tuning, the fan belt needs tightening, or some other repair or adjustment needs to be made. You recognize these signs because you've learned to be sensitive to your car. You know what a smooth, trouble-free ride feels like, and you are ever alert to rattles and clinks.

In the same way, you need to stay alert, receptive, and sensitive to your own needs and those of your lover. If you growl and snap at everyone who approaches you, ask yourself what's going on. What's fueling your negative mood? Are you angry, upset, or perhaps afraid of something in your relationship?

If you find your typically energetic partner slumped listlessly in a chair, that's your clue that something is wrong. Rather than chew out our partner for being lazy, take a minute to check out what's happened. Did the boss pounce on her at work, or did he lose the election for vice-president of his club?

When you're aware of your feelings—both positive and negative—and those of your partner, you are in a much better position to give and receive love. By catching problems early, you become more successful at resolving disputes and preventing them from becoming huge, seemingly insurmountable problems.

TODAY

How is your partner feeling today? Notice all the signals—body posture, vitality level, strength of voice, eye contact, desire to talk with you or respond to you. Is your partner's engine running as well as it can? If not, make whatever adjustments you can so that your lover feels appreciated. If she's feeling low after a hard day at work, tell her you know she's the greatest. If he's feeling old and unattractive, tell him he's appealing to you in every way—and mean it!

Share Feelings

One of the most fragile aspects of a love relationship is trust. Without trust we tend to play our cards close to the vest. With it we're likely to blossom in the sunshine.

To trust our lovers, we need to be willing to take some risks, willing to open our hearts and minds to the unexpected or the unknown, willing to accept a little heartache and disappointment.

Healthy lovers know life offers no guarantees. So why worry? Yesterday is gone, and no one knows what tomorrow holds in store. The truth is, today is really all we have and we'll probably have more than enough to challenge us.

Some of the bigger risks we can take are to tell our lovers how we feel today, what is important to us at a given moment, and who our "true selves" really are. These can be pretty scary subjects when our discussions have been limited to what brand of fertilizer to put on the lawn, or whether to have orange juice or grapefruit juice for breakfast. When we close down and stop being vulnerable, we stop recognizing who we are and what we feel. We begin to wither inside. When we stop letting our partners know what is important to us, we are really saying that they aren't very important to us. We are also depriving our partners of the opportunity to love us the way we would like to be loved.

One way to start taking some risks is to share our feelings about a recent event. We might talk about the disturbing dream we had last night or our sorrow over some loss we have recently had. Sharing a feeling with our partners gives them a chance to be empathic and to respond in kind.

Trust is something that has to be built slowly over time. As we begin to feel more confident about our lovers, we can share more deeply and reconnect once more.

TODAY

Recall a recent event you felt strongly about and share the event and your feelings about it with your partner. Ask your partner to respond in kind. 49

Humor

Irritations are almost inevitable in daily life. When we feel irritated, disappointed, or downright angry, we can make a choice. We can let things escalate into World War III, or we can find a way to find humor in the situation.

One Saturday morning Diane went off to the office she shared with her husband, Mark, to work on an upcoming presentation. She headed for the office, ready and eager to get her work done so she could get back home and be with her family. Lugging her briefcase, a stack of heavy books, and ten other things to the office door, she shoved her key into the lock. Twist, jam, punch, reinsert, scream . . . nothing happened. She tried again and again. No success. She even walked around the building and tried another door. So intense was her frustration that she didn't even realize she was using the wrong key.

Loading up the car again and driving back home, Diane realized she had two choices. One, take a baseball bat to Mark for neglecting to tell her the locks had been changed. Two, see how ridiculous she must have looked kicking and screaming at the locked door.

Oftentimes we let small things ruin our day. Our blaming, shaming, and accusing ways only alienate our lover and create distance between us. Relying on a sense of humor, looking for the folly in our actions, and letting minor irritations roll off our backs brings perspective to our lives and keeps our love intact..

When life goes bananas, we can make banana bread.

TODAY

When a minor irritation flares up today, fight the urge to snap or bark. First, take a deep breath. Next, instead of firing back with criticism or blame, count to ten very slowly and find the hidden humor in your situation.

Appreciation

Many of us dash off in the morning, barely stopping to tell our partners good-bye.

At night, we turn the key in the lock breathlessly. No warm greeting awaits us. The kids have their noses buried in a book or their eyes glued to the TV set. Our partners are nowhere in sight.

After several months of this routine, Neil announced that he was going to buy a dog. "What on earth for?" Corinne asked, astonished by Neil's sudden declaration. "Don't you think we have enough chaos in our live?!"

"I'm tired of coming home and you're not even here to say, 'Hello! How was your day?' At least a dog would wag its tail," Neil replied, not attempting to hide his feelings of rejection.

While Corinne didn't like Neil's solution, she realized he was right; she had begun taking his coming and going for granted. He deserved to know that his presence at home was appreciated and that she was happy to have him near her once again.

Make loving good-byes and hellos an important, special part of each day. Wrapping your arms and legs around your partner in an octopus hug, whispering "I love you" in one ear and "I'll be waiting for you" in the other, or escorting your partner to the car for a lingering kiss are all good send-offs. Helping your partner into a comfortable chair at the end of the day, offering a refreshing drink at the door, massaging tired feet or aching temples, or giving a quick back rub can melt away the day's tensions and show how glad you are to have your lover back home by your side.

TODAY

Tune in to your partner's need to feel loved, desired, and appreciated by you. When you part in the morning, do so with a long, loving kiss and some tender words that express your love. Greet your partner with love and appreciation at the end of the day.

Take Time for Each Other

What catches your eye and makes you take a second
look at that man or woman walking past you? Is it
the fit of her clingy sweater or his tight-fitting jeans?

Whatever those elements that make hearts pound
and palms sweat, tiny electrical impulses go zapping
and sparking their way straight to our sexual nerve
center. Bull's-eye.

All of us want to feel attractive and able to turn
our partner's head. Though we may have gained a
few pounds, lost a little hair, or sagged a touch in
important places, we still want to feel that we are irre-
sistable.

Stan and Allison tackled this subject by setting
aside two days a month as "Date Night." Not rain,
nor snow, nor sick kids kept these two from their
commitment to spend "their" evening alone.

Twice a month, Stan and Allison get spiffed up,
don sexy clothes, and go out to enjoy each other's
company. Whether for a moonlight walk in the park,

54

or buying a chili dog at the Dairy Queen, they act as if it is the most romantic thing they've ever done. They make each date feel like a first date. They flirt and tease, steal kisses, and stroke each other lovingly, as the mood strikes.

Going out of your way to look nice for your lover and creating a special time for yourselves helps you put excitement, romance, and newfound sexual energy into your relationship.

TODAY

Go out on a date with your lover once a week. Choose a night when neither of you has any other commitments. No matter what comes up, don't break your date. Make "Date Night" your priority.

Get a Little Crazy

Dave drove home Friday evening, tired and a little punchy. It had been a long, exhausting week. Having arrived home first, Stephanie saw Dave's car ease into the driveway. She quickly hid behind the couch, and when Dave came in she quietly waited for him. As he approached, she jumped out and began meowing and rubbing up against his leg.

At first, Dave was startled by Stephanie's strange welcome. But within seconds he joined her and began barking like a dog and chasing Stephanie under the table, over the counter, and around the furniture. After a while they were sprawled out on the dining room floor, laughing in each other's arms.

Dave and Stephanie's playfulness let them release their emotions and became the springboard to a very enjoyable weekend.

Few of us honestly remember how to play. Here are some tips to get you going again. First, devise some sort of signal to let your partner know that you're in a playful mood.

Next, get agreement that your partner will join in the fun. It's important to build in emotional safety by eliminating any sense of competition. Loving playfulness is not about winning a medal or one-upping the other person.

The shared experience of acting unpredictable, childlike, and zany demonstrates that we have more than one side. And it encourages us to be lovable and fun-loving.

TODAY

Signal to your partner that you want to be silly and playful today. If you have trouble coming up with an idea, try lip-syncing to a song in an exaggerated fashion. Play it up for all it's worth!

Self-revelation

Oftentimes most of the conversations we have with our partner end up being about mundane household matters. Did you take out the garbage? How much will it cost to replace the broken window in the kitchen?

When we limit our conversations to everyday details, it's generally because we feel like strangers and we're uncomfortable disclosing anything more than our most superficial concerns.

It is important to share your feelings, thoughts, and beliefs with your partner. Knowing each other intimately—in all your fear and frailty—feeds love and allows it to grow and deepen. Start small so you'll feel safe and so you won't baffle your partner by revealing yourself all at once.

Here are two lists of topics you can use to start a conversation with your partner. List A is fairly light, and List B is a bit bolder.

List A: Talk about a favorite schoolteacher, the

best movie you've ever seen, a man or woman you truly admire, or how you survived your teenage years.

List B: Talk about your beliefs about a life hereafter, your most embarrassing moment, the things you like most about your partner, or your personal goals for the future.

Here are a few simple conversation rules:

- Never start a sentence with why. It makes some people feel defensive.

- Conversation is an exchange—both are responsible for keeping the ball rolling.

- Lulls in the conversation are acceptable and sometimes even a welcome pause.

TODAY

Pick two items from List A to talk about today. You need spend only five or ten minutes on each item. If you're feeling brave, go for the daily double and also take two questions from List B.

Small Things Count

Keeping the feeling of being in love with your partner
can present a challenge. Feeling romantic is tough
after working all day, meeting with your child's
English teacher about that D, and doing the laundry.

Collapsing into bed at the end of a hard day, we
may find it difficult to muster the energy to engage in
any kind of meaningful, intimate activity. Like the
sign in the window of O'Reilly's bar, we're closed for
the night!

Being in love is partly a state of mind and partly
our use of words and actions. When you treat your
lover as the most important person in your life, you
declare your intention to stay in love. You choose to
make your lover a priority. In turn, your thoughts,
words, and actions flow naturally from this commitment.

Still, being in love takes some effort. And often
it's the small things that speak the loudest.

Bringing home a handful of flowers you picked

by the side of the road, giving your lover a homemade card, or shooing the kids off to bed early so you can snuggle and watch a favorite TV program alone, all demonstrate your commitment to keeping your love alive. Likewise, arranging a weekend away from home, staying overnight at a bed-and-breakfast inn, or sending the kids off to stay with friends for a night show how serious love is to you.

TODAY

Make a list of little things you can do or say to demonstrate your love and appreciation for your partner. Something as simple as rinsing out the bathroom sink after shaving or taking out the garbage when it's his turn lets your lover know that you care. Start with a list if fifteen items and add at least one new item to the list each day.

DAY 30
Creative Loving

Most of us let our love life fall into certain routines and patterns. These habits may bring some regularity to sex, yet this predictability can get boring. And nothing does more to kill the initial excitement of love than boredom.

What are some simple ways to add spice and variety to your lovemaking? Consider these options:

- Throw away the schedule and make love at different times or in different rooms. Who knows? You might find afternoon love a bit more exciting than love at midnight.

- Take a drive to your old make-out spot. The nostalgia may just rekindle some hot ideas.

- Swap houses with friends for the weekend or plan an evening at a bed and breakfast inn. It's amazing how new surroundings can give you a different perspective on life.

- Nothing's more romantic than the twinkling of Christmas lights and the crackling of a fire. Who cares if it's a cool night in July? String up a set of lights and build a fire in the fireplace. Dust off the sleeping bag or spread cozy blankets on the floor and you've got the perfect setting for love.

• If all else fails, a pillow fight, having a tickling contest, or engaging in a hand of strip poker are all sure to prove fun and, no doubt, stimulating.

Remember, you don't have to think for hours to come up with a creative, romantic setting or activity. Just about anything that allows you to break out of stale, dull routines will have a surprising effect.

TODAY

Pick one of the items listed in today's reading and plan when and where you'll carry it out. If none of these are right for you, think of some other ways to break out of your old habits and routines.

Perfect Gifts for Any Occasion